Go-Kart Go!

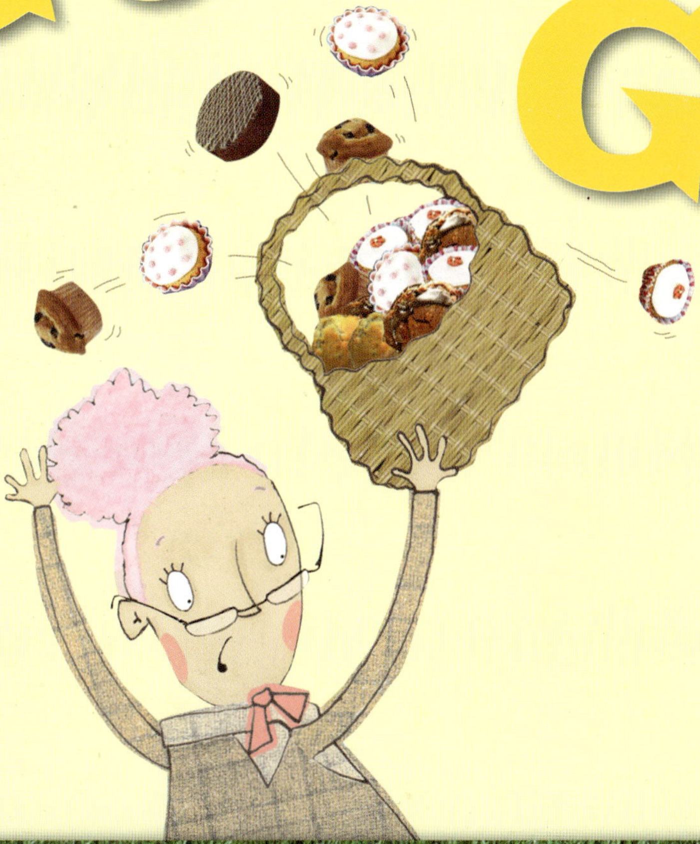

Written by Jill Atkins
Illustrated by Mark Chambers

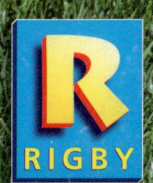

Chris and Kate found some wheels.
"Let's make a go-kart!" said Kate.
"This box could be the cockpit!" said Chris.

"Can I be Captain?" asked Kate.
"If you like," said Chris.
"Three, two, one … GO!"

They shot to the corner.
"STOP!" screamed Chris.
"We cannot stop," shouted Kate.
"We forgot to make brakes!"

They saw Mrs Cross carrying cakes.
"Look out!" yelled Chris.
Whoops! The cakes fell into the go-kart.

Mrs Cross was very cross!
"Come back!" she shouted.
But the go-kart kept going.

Soon they came to the market.
"Keep back!" yelled Chris.
"We cannot stop!"

The crowd scattered as the go-kart crashed into kites, coats and carrots.

"Quack! Quack!" said the ducks.
"Come back!" shouted a man.
But the go-kart kept going.

A hammock fell from a hook.
"Where are we going?" called Kate.

Chris grabbed a scarlet scarf.
"This is crazy!" called Chris.
"I like it!" laughed Kate.

They crashed into crates and cartons. Confetti and cornflakes, crackers and crisps fell into the go-kart.

Then the go-kart hit a kerb.
Whoosh! It flew out of control.

All at once, the go-kart stopped and the crowd stopped too.

A man came running from a field.
"This is just what I am looking for," he said.
"Can you come back on Saturday?"

So, on Saturday, Chris and Kate took their go-kart to the carnival. It was the star of the show!